The Bloke's Guide to Brilliant Cooking and How to Impress Women

Blokes don't cook, they construct!

The do-it-yourself guide for the two most important things in a bloke's life:
the love of great food and impressing women

Jim O'Connor

To order additional copies of this book, contact:
Xlibris
1-800-455-039
www.xlibris.com.au
Orders@Xlibris.com.au

The Blokes' Guide to Brilliant Cooking and How to Impress Women

The 'do-it-yourself' guide for two of the most important things in a bloke's life: the love of good food and impressing women! If you want to learn how to cook brilliant meals using the knowledge, imagination, and instincts you already have whilst simultaneously learning how to impress women then read on. If not, it's OK. We won't tell anyone.

Acknowledgements

For me, the most gratitude must go to my beautiful wife for her believing in my dreams and for putting up with me and them until they were realised. She inspires me in ways she probably doesn't even realise. To my oldest friends and family who have taught me much over dinner and red wine, I say. Last but not least, I want to acknowledge and thank my children, for helping me discover the joy of playing with possibilities and fantastic ideas. Hopefully, one day they will understand just how much they helped inspire me to pursue the dream.

Jim O'Connor

Every Bloke's Most Important Lesson

"Trust "The Code" always trust "The Code""

The Original Bloke
The first bloke and Originator of The Code,
A Man of Mystery and Legend

'The Code'

This book is dedicated to the wisdom of Blokes as preserved in 'The Code' (yes, ladies it does exist), its authors who dedicated their lives to recording and thus preserving that wisdom, and to the Cleverest Blokes of all time who inspired that wisdom.

Trust the Code, Guys, always Trust the Code

OB

Special Request

All the information in this book comes to you straight out of 'The Code'. Knowing this I'd like to ask of you a simple favour. 'The Code' has remained secret for a very long time, and we in the brotherhood want it to continue to remain secret for another very long time. Knowing this I kindly request that you don't share what you learn within these pages with anyone who is not a bloke or honorary bloke or blokette. To do so could undermine the very ancient "Way of the Bloke".

Special Note

This book represents the first time in history that any part of 'The Code' has been made available to the public. To all the brothers who dedicated their lives to its protection and secrecy, we sincerely apologise.

However, due to dwindling memberships and economic constraints caused by the subprime crash the Brotherhood of Blokes have with great regret determined it is better to publish and thus guarantee the perpetuation of 'The Code' than to see it fade from knowledge.

We only ask any of you who may read these words support us in keeping it secret and thus preserve the integrity of 'The Way of the Bloke', as described in the pages of 'The Code'.

Disclaimer

All persons seemingly identified by the material in this book will deny any knowledge, engagement, association, or experience of 'The Code', its practices, products, and services. In short, they will claim it doesn't exist! Further to that any persons seemingly identified in this book are fictitious and, if confronted, will also deny any relationship with the materials here in with.

Impressiveness

An Impressive bloke's purpose is to be impressive
Con T B

"Impressive blokes cook without a net.
Recipe books are for sissies."

Con T B
A hard bloke, the ultimate bloke's bloke
from The Book of Legends

Impressive Blokes cook without a net.

As you read through this book, you will discover that this is not a 'how to follow someone else's impressive recipe' book. This is a 'how to cook impressively' book. The reason we chose not to put recipes in this book is because recipe books are other people's ideas and cooking creations. It's not 'the way of the bloke' as it's written in 'The Code' to copy other people's great ideas. Following someone else's recipe in order to make yourself look impressive is not cool; it is effectively culinary plagiarism and that just isn't "Code". Being an impressive bloke is about standing out, being authentic and above all original. There's nothing wrong with following recipes of course, as long they're, yours.

By working your way through the concepts in this book, you will discover how to cook without the safety net of someone else's cooking ideas. You will be able to create impressive meals from nothing more than an idea inside your head. You'll be able to write your own original recipe book with as many brilliant dinners in it as you can possibly imagine. Nothing could be more satisfying, and nothing could be more impressive.

You will also come to learn that you already know more than enough to plan, prepare, produce, and plate up an impressive meal. Anything you don't know that you may need to know, we will show you. What we are going to do is show you how to pull what you already know together in an impressive way. We are going to show you how to use what you already know to create inspired plans, to guide the whole process from beginning to end with sharp instincts and deliver it all with imaginative execution. What's more we're going to show you how to put the super-secret into your cooking that no chef school can teach you. We're going to show you how to put Heart into your cooking.

So are you ready to meet the Blokes' Guide challenge. Are you ready to test yourself in the kitchen? Are you ready to learn how to walk into any kitchen anywhere in the world, armed with nothing more than your, head, instincts, imagination, heart and hands, and start chopping, cutting, mixing, and plating up genius meals without the safety of a recipe book. Are you ready to do what all the great blokes have always done throughout history and to cook without a net? If you're up for it, then read on. If you're not, learn to live dangerously and just have a go?

PS

Before you go on, let me remind you about a bloke's most important lesson.

'Trust the code; always trust 'The Code'

Yours

OB

Pan-seared tuna with sesame seed crust

Are you ready to cook without a net?

You Can Do this all you have to do is

Trust the Code

Follow the steps

Think like a bloke

Have a go

Boom your done

"Recipe books are full of other people's ideas about cooking. Following someone else's recipe is like culinary plagiarism and that just simply isn't impressive. It's not 'the way of the bloke'. Do it your way"

Dean M
A man who knew how to do it. his way.
From the book of legends

Grilled Tuna
Ginger and Shallots

Are you ready to trust
yourself and cook
without a net?

You know you want to!

It's simple just

Believe,

See

Do!

Wanky Facts

Before humans could write, they used their heads, instincts, imagination, hearts and hands to do everything including cooking. Because they had to.

A Moment in Cooking History

The First-known Recipe

The truth is it probably happened as soon as humans started writing. However, our earliest surviving copy was a recipe for dried figs written on a clay tablet in ancient Mesopotamia.

Most ancient recipes were used by healers to remember their special combinations of medicinal herbs.

The first recipe book was probably written by a Greek Sicilian named Archestratus in 350 bc. Electric guitar legend Jimmy Hendrix's last meal was a tuna sandwich.

Secret Women Business

Women love a bloke who loves to impress them

Brilliant Cooking

"Brilliant cooking is what happens when your head, instincts, imagination and heart get on the same plate and tell your hands what to do in kitchen".

Antony C,
uber-legendary cook for really, important blokes and blokettes,
From the Book of Legends

Are your ready to be simply brilliant?

Get your head, instincts, imagination and heart to agree and then tell your hands what to do and boom your in the B Zone

Antony, C

Uber-Legendary-Cook to really important blokes and blokettes

From the book of Legends

Brilliant cooking

You might be thinking, you have to learn to cook like a chef to impress like a chef. Well, that could be a problem if you aren't already a chef. Fortunately, you don't have to be a chef to impress like one. What you have to do, however, is use what you already know in a very impressive way. By learning the secrets in this book, you are going to learn how to cook unlimited brilliant meals and impress like a chef by cooking and thinking the way a bloke naturally thinks, that is, like a bloke.

One of the greatest cooking blokes of all time Antony C (a legendary cook to kings and queens in days gone by) said, 'Brilliant cooking is what happens when your head, instincts, imagination, and your heart get together on the same plate and tell your hands what to do in the kitchen'. This book is going to show how anyone of any skill level can cook brilliantly if they learn how to do just that. To get started, you need to realize that each part of your brilliant cooking partnership has a job to do. The head has a job; the imagination has a job. The instincts have a job, the heart has a job and the hands have a job.

In the following pages, you are going to be shown how to tap into your bloke's DNA and perform wonders in the kitchen by getting your head, instincts, imagination, and heart together, so they can tell your hands what to do. You don't have to worry about anything. It's all been taken care of for you by some of the greatest blokes of all time, as written in 'The Code'. You just have to read, follow the steps, enjoy, and then just have a go at it yourself.

You will learn that you already know enough to cook impressively. You will learn that by using your head and thinking the way a bloke naturally thinks, you can easily organise what you already know into a brilliant meal. You will learn how to bring together your instincts and your imagination so that you can plan, prepare, and construct unlimited seriously impressive meals easily. But we don't want to just stop there because you will also learn how to add major X factor to your meals.

Oh, by the way, you will also learn a few words of advice about that other obsession blokes seem to have; how to impress women. So, pour yourself a cup of your favorite beverage settle into a comfy chair read on.

OB

PS

Here's your first tip on impressing women. Learn how to connect, your head, your instincts, your imagination, heart and hands all together and you're well on your way to impressing the woman you want to impress. Women love a bloke who has it all together. Think about it?

PPS

Also learn to use her name like you love it. She'll love it.

Are you ready trust your head, instincts, imagination and heart? Are you ready to get fully connected Bloke?

Don't worry, you already know more than enough to give it a good crack

Al

Head

"The heads job is to organize what you already know brilliantly"
(Al E)

You don't need cooking lessons,
you need thinking lessons

Al E,
uber-smart bloke and seriously good thinker
from The Book of Answers

The only problem you have is the way you think about the problem you think you have. So, change the way you think.

Al. E
Seriously smart bloke
from The Book of Answers

Ask yourself what do
you need to change
in your thinking
to think brilliantly
about cooking?

Think about it?

You don't need cooking lessons. You need thinking lessons

So how do you get your instincts, your imagination, and your head all on the same page so they can tell your hands what to do anywhere let alone in the kitchen? Well, it isn't by sending you to chef school? The first step in "connecting up" all your cooking parts is to begin by changing the way you think about cooking.

Now we don't want you thinking I'm someone who isn't a chef pretending to be a chef. That'll just end in a train wreck. No, we want you to, trust your bloke DNA and start thinking the way a bloke naturally thinks, and that is like a bloke? If you think, you don't have enough knowledge or experience to be able to cook impressively, you won't even start. But if you believe you already have more than enough know how and experience to do the job, then problem solved. That is one of the first things we are going to show you. If you already are an amazing cook and you want to be more amazing, then the answer is the same. Change the way you think by asking yourself how I can use what I already know to create even more amazing meals.

For those of you who haven't cooked a lot and who have doubt, believe this. If you have ever eaten a good meal, watched a good meal being cooked, if you have ever boiled an egg, cooked a chop, tossed a salad, or cooked toast, you have more than enough experience to cook impressively. if you can look, listen, touch, taste, and smell, if you know what you like to eat, if have ever looked at a plate of food and gone wow I want a piece of that, then you have all the judgment, instincts, and imagination needed to cook impressively. If you can hold a spoon, mix a bowl of stuff, turn heat on and turn it off, if you can chop without losing your fingers, then you have all the skills necessary to cook impressively. If you can say yes to most of these, then you are right to go.

Think about this, what's normal cooking anyway? Isn't it just planning, preparing, chopping, mixing, heating, or cooling food and putting it on a plate? How hard can that be? But this book isn't about normal cooking; this book is about brilliant cooking. So, think about this what's brilliant cooking? Well, that's just as easy; brilliant cooking is normal cooking but with the colours, flavours, textures in the right balance, as well as with some fancy accessories thrown in.

Now, I want to make an important point. Don't confuse brilliant cooking with chef cooking. Chef cooking is uber-brilliant cooking. Chef cooking is brilliant cooking with extra special colours, flavours, and textures, as well as fancy processes and fancy accessories. This book is about impressing like a chef by using what you already know. We will leave chef-type cooking for the Advanced Blokes' Guide. The problem isn't what you know or don't know; the problem is how you use what you know. You have more than enough information in your head to produce a million brilliant meals; all you have to do is use it in a clever way.

OB

Think about it. Brilliant cooking is just normal cooking with special colours, flavours, textures, and some fancy accessories?

Leo DV
Uber Creative Bloke
From the book of legends

Take a classic, pimp it up with some fancy colours, textures and accessories and bam you've constructed something brilliant. Think about it!

You know more
than you think
you know.

The secret is to use what
you already know in an
impressive way.

By letting your head,
instincts, imagination
and heart tell your
hands what to do

Wanky Facts

Everything that is created by a person (not by accident or by an animal) begins as a thought in someone's head.

A Moment in Cooking History

It is likely that the first cooked meal was discovered by accident and was simply a dead beast found lying on the ground by some poor hungry cave man after a wild fire somewhere between 500,000 and 1,500,000 years ago. The threat of starvation will do that.

However, it was only about 125,000 years ago that humans learned to control fire for cooking purposes. I guess we are slow learners.

Secret Women Business

Women love a bloke who thinks like them. Think like a girl; get the girl! Think about it?

Copyright Jim O'Connor

"Smart Blokes think Backwards"

Sherlock. H

A bloke who knew how to think backward brilliantly

From the book of Answers

Smart Blokes Think Backwards

One of the cleverest backward thinkers of all time Sherlock knew that starting where you want to be at the end and working backwards through the logical steps until you arrive where you are is the best way to deduce all the steps from the beginning to the end. Follow this strategy and I promise you won't miss a step.

So here is how to do backward thinking best. First things first. The head work. This starts with sitting in a comfy chair with your favourite beverage and doing the backward thinking. Her's how it runs. Start with a picture in your head of what your final creation looks like on the plate on the table in front of your favourite lady. This is called the table work. Then imagine the step before that. We blokes in the brotherhood call this the pre-table work. You know the last-minute polishing and finishing of the final product. Then imagine the plate work. That is the placing and presenting of each part of your culinary creation onto the plate in a creative way. Then imagine the pre-plate work, that is the hot work and the cold work and then cooling mixing work. Then, imagine the bench work, such as chopping, pealing, mixing, and preparing the work site. Imagine the pre-bench work, such as unpacking the raw materials and getting them ready for pre-fabrication. Then imagine the site work, you know the setting up of the work site and tidying up the space, setting out the bowls, boards and bins, laying out the, pots pans and tools. Then imagine the pre-site work or going to the shops and buying up a storm. Now, imagine the step before that or the head-work. In other words, the planning. I think you get it.

Thinking backwards from where you want to be to where you are means you will be able to work out the steps, the timing, the processes, the tools and equipment, the quantities and amounts before you get started. You'll know exactly how you need to set up your work site with your tools to one side, your raw materials to the other and a place for your waste. Oh, by the way it helps if you right the steps down as you work from where you want to end up to where you already are. Though when you master this craft you'll be able to do it all in your head.

Now think about this neat trick. If you write down the backward steps from where you want to end up to where you are now, then all you need to do is turn your list upside down and you now have in perfect order the steps you need to take to get from where you are to where you want to be all laid out in forward thinking order. Mind you if you follow this method strictly you will have to learn to read right to left and upside down. It's not that hard really. Or you could simply read your list from bottom to top instead of top to bottom. Whatever strategy you choose is fine. I am sure you'll work it out.

I know this can seem a bit overwhelming at first thought but master the craft of backward thinking and you simply won't, go wrong. It isn't as hard as it seems. It just takes a bit of practice. Besides in true trust the code style your great uncle Sherlock has provided you with a simple to follow backward thinking planner on the next few pages to make this process super easy. Have a look at it. It's simple and it works.

OB

Backward thinking planner
Smart Blokes Think Backwards
Sherlock H

Stage	Pictures What you want in your head	Processes See the processes	Tools and Materials 1. Tools 2. Temperatures 3. Timings 4. Materials 5. Processes
Table work			
Pre-table work			
Plate work			
Pre-plate work			
Hot work			
Cold work			
Bench work			
Pre-bench work			
Site work			
Pre-site work			
Head work			

Thinking Backwards

Table Work.
Place bowl on the table with a flourish

Pre-Table Work
Finishing touches
Clean up and polish finished product

Plate work
Place salad in the bottom of the bowl
Put avocado on the side of the bowl
Put balls on the side of the bowl,
Plop on beetroot puree. Toss on some chopped olives

Pre-Plate work
All ingredients are laid out ready for plating

Bench work
Organize all your prepared materials ready for plating Take hot-works off
the heat rest ready for plating (the Balls, Arancini balls made with polenta)
Cold works Veg) are, chopped, sliced, diced and prepared for plating.
Beetroot puree blitzed, salts, spiced or herbed, to taste, ready for plating.

Hot work
Polenta balls are deep fried to crisp golden brown. Polenta is balled, and
cheese is placed inside the balls Polenta is rested and cooled ready for
balling
Polenta is mixed with butter, salt to taste and hot water, then heated ready
for balling
Cheese is chopped ready for putting into Arancini balls

Pre-Bench Work
Groceries are un-packed and laid out ready for bench work Wrappers
removed Rubbish cleared away

Site Works
Work Site is set up Tools are laid out.
Waste receptacles are laid out
Bowls for organising cooked and prepared materials are laid out.
Back from the shops and food is unpacked ready or laying out.

Pre-Site Works
Go to shops buy ingredients

Head Work
Turn the backward planner upside down and write your list of ingredients
and list of tools and processes
Backward planning completed
Work through the backward thinking steps
Pick up a pen imagine finished product on the plate on the table.
Work backwards to figure out the steps, processes, times and tools
Figure out where you are and where you want to be

Copyright Jim O'Connor

Have a look at this.
De-construct it by thinking backwards.
Write down the steps using the backward thinking planner now. Reconstruct it by working
Give it a go yourself

Table Work

Pre-Table Work

Plate Work

Pre-Plate Work

Bench Work

Hot Work

Cold Work

Pre-Bench Work

Site Work

Pre-Site Work

Head Work

Backward thinking It's what super smart blokes do.

Sherlock
Uber-Smart Bloke and Backward Thinking Expert
From the book of Answers

Wanky Facts

Before recipe books were written cooks had to think backwards to cook every meal they made. They had to see it in their heads first and then work out the steps from where they are to where they need to be and then just do it.

A Moment in Cooking History

Controversy surrounds the humble pasta. Some say it is likely an Italianised version of Asian noodles and was introduced into Italy Marco Polo in the 13th Century.

However, the basic ingredients of flour, egg and water is a common combination that was used by peasants all around the world where ever flour was grown. What do you think?

Basil has been found in the tombs of Ancient Egyptian Mummies. It was used as an ingredient in embalming.

Secret Women Business

Women love a bloke who can work out the steps by himself.

Instincts

"The instincts' job is to guide what you already know so it looks, smells, tastes, sounds and feels brilliant"
(Jean GS)

"Smart blokes trust their animal."

Jean GS,
A bloke who lived wild,
from The Book of Legends

The problem with civilised man is he has forgotten that he's just an animal, and sadly he has forgotten to think with his animal.

Jean G,
A bloke who lived wild,
from The Book of Legends

Are you ready to trust your animal?

Smart blokes trust their animal

Smart blokes throughout history have always known that their animal instincts (animal for short) knows best. Why you ask, simple because he's designed that way! Your animal knows in an instant what looks good. He knows what tastes good, he knows what sounds, smells, and feels good. He also knows when things don't look, sound, smell, taste, and feel good, and he will tell you just as quickly if you're prepared to listen. By learning to listen to your animal, you will be able to use what you know in an impressive way. You were given animal senses and instincts for a reason so use them. Your animal is boss!

This section of this book is about getting you back in touch with your animal, so you can use your animal instincts to judge if things are right or not? The trick for doing this is simple enough. Look at it with your eyes, touch it with your fingers, taste it with your tongue, smell it with your nose, and yes listen to it with your ears, and if after all that if your animal is wagging his tail, then you can be confident that you're on to something good.

The more your animal wags his tail, gets all excited, and salivates, the better the thing you're cooking is probably going to be. On the other hand, if your animal isn't wagging his tail, if he is disinterested, or if he is going I'm not really sure about this or that, then you need to listen because he's telling you that something just isn't right, and you're heading for a bunch of disappointment.

I am going to show you a secret test that we in the bloke-hood have known about for a long time and it will get you back in touch with your inner animal. By learning how to use this test, you will be able to judge whether what you're planning is good, great, or indifferent. You'll be able to decide whether your production process is working and what to do about it if it isn't. You'll be able to create great plating and presentation using your instincts. You'll be able to tell if the balance of colours, flavours, and textures is working or not. You will be able to tell if something is cooked or not; the benefits of thinking with your animal are endless. In fact, using this test will always leave you in good shape all the time every time. So learn it well.

The test is called 'The Great Crap Test' or GCT for short, and was first thought up by that wild man of wild men, Jean G. Now I want you to pay attention, so you don't miss it. This is how it the GCT works. "If something looks great, smells great, tastes, sounds, and feels great then it is great. Which means that if something looks crap, sounds, smells, tastes, and feels crap, it is crap?" Too simple really!

The GCT can be applied to every part of the cooking process from beginning to end. Whatever stage you are at, look at it and ask your animal if it looks good or not. Listen to it and see if he says it sounds right; get your fingers out and touch it to see if it feels right. Use your mouth and taste it to see if it tastes right. Use your nose to smell it and decide if it smells right.

If what you are doing gets a big nod from all your animal instincts, then you have yourself a very impressive dinner. In other words, if your animal is salivating and wagging his tail with excitement, then you have got yourself an impressive meal. If, on the other hand, he isn't getting interested, then ask yourself which of your animal's senses are unhappy. Is it the eyes, ears, nose, tongue, and fingers? Once you have figured out which of your animal's senses are being let down, then change things so that part of your meal gets him excited

Have a look at the chart below. It will help you use the GCT with complete ease and effectiveness. This simple idea can be adapted to suit thousands of applications. The trick is to ask yourself what I have to change about my meal to increase my greatness score and decrease my crappiness score. Remember, the trick is to ask your animal which sense is unsatisfied, and then change that bit until he is happy.

Think about it?

OB

The Great Crap Test (GCT for short)
Smart Blokes Trust their Animal
Jean GS

Sense	Greatness	Crapiness	Write what changes you are going to do to get your animal wagging his tail.	
Looks	/10	/10	Look	
Sounds	/10	/10	Sound	
Smells	/10	/10	Smell	
Tastes	/10	/10	Taste	
Feels	/10	/10	Feel	

Try this exercise. Look at the two meals below and score them for greatness and crappiness using the GCT. Then decide what you would do to make them less crappy and more great.

Great or not great, that is the question.
Let your animal decide

Crap or not crap, that is the question?
Let your animal decide

You can apply the GCT to anything from planning to production. Remember you want a high score for greatness and a low score for crappiness. Any score below a 6 for greatness and above a 4 for crappiness you need to worry about because your animal isn't happy. Ask yourself what I have to do to raise the greatness score above 6 and drop the crappiness scored below 4 so that my animal can be happy again.

Be ruthless. The biggest mistake that people make when using the GCT is they get too wimpy. Don't get too sold on your ideas and refuse to change them. Remember 'your animal is boss'. If he isn't wagging his tail, then you need to trust him, and you need to make the necessary changes until he does.

As you become expert at using the GCT, you'll start doing it in your head, so you won't need to write anything down. You'll just look at stuff ask your animal what he thinks, and then he will give you the answer straight up. Too easy! The important part of this lesson is that you learn to let your animal senses inform your judgment. This is how you will prevent your head from confusing your hands by being too clever.

If It Looks great

smells great

Sounds great

Tastes great

Feels great

It is great!

Wanky Facts

Before there were cooking advice columns and hi-tech cooking measuring and mixing devices, people cooked using their animal instincts. Why, you ask? They had to!

A big impression is what happens when the imagination and the eyes, ears, tongue, fingers, and nose get excited all at the same time.

Something to Think About

Have you ever noticed that when chef's cook on TV, they almost never follow a recipe? There's a reason for that. They are totally in touch with their animal.

A Moment in Food History

The world's first fast food was fish and chips in the 1800s. But the world's first fast food store owners were probably soap manufacturers in Britain who used coconut and their soap kettles to deep fry fish and potatoes.

Secret Women Business

Women love a bloke who has good instincts.

Senses

"The senses job is to wow the mind, excite the emotions, and surprise the imagination"
(David. C)

"Master Blokes mess with your senses"

David C,
A master of messing with the senses
from The Book of Magic

Master Blokes mess with your senses

I was once speaking to a very clever bloke who knew a lot about making a huge impression by messing with the senses. He said this. There is a simple truth about cooking that we sometimes take for granted, or for that matter, we overlook all together. We recognize great food is great because of how much it messes with our senses, in a good way that is. What this means he went on to explain is when our imagination goes wow, and our minds are surprised, and emotions get all excited we know we're having a really good time. When it comes to brilliant cooking that's the goal. You must aim to excite the eyes, make the nose go I love smelling that, get the tongue and mouth salivating and wanting more. You must surprise the imagination if you really want to take the show to the next level. When it comes to making the midnight show this is a must.

With that in mind and whilst we're still on the subject of thinking with your animal its time to devote a bit of attention to taste. To get the whole taste experience worked out you really have to get your tongue around the food you're preparing and see what your animal does. Now depending on whether your' animal is happy or not will determine what you do next.

If when you wrap your tongue around your food, your' animal is saying, that is fabulous, give me more then you're right to go. If on the other hand your animal says ooh yuck or I'm not sure then you can use a variation of the Great, Crap Test to decide what to do to fix it. The variation test is the Great Crap Test for Tongues and it works the same way as the GCT, but the criteria are different. In the GCT for Tongues your trying to max flavour. Now some of you might know already but for those who don't there are only five flavours you really need to worry about. Sweet, salty, sour, bitter and umami. When it comes to these flavours most are self-explanatory. However, Umami is a bit of a tricky one. The best way to understand it is Umami is what happens in your brain when fishy, meaty, herby, earthy, proteins have a party on your taste buds and add a whole bunch of deliciousness to your eating experience.

Now to make it a bit more interesting your tongue lets you know about texture as well. Texture matters. So here is the thing. There are certain textures we naturally like that go with certain flavours. Now I could go on and bore you with a whole bunch or stuff about texture or I could just tell you to listen to your animal. Guess what the answer is? That's right, I'm going to tell you to just listen to your animal and he will not lead you astray.

Now to help get you started have a look at the GCT for Tongue on the next page and have a go at tasting and texturing a whole bunch of dinners and listen to what your animal has to say.

Yours

OB

The Great Crap Test for The Tongue (Taste & Texture)

Flavour	Greatness	Crapiness	Write what changes you are going to do to get your animal wagging his tail.
Sweet	/10	/10	
Salty	/10	/10	
Sour	/10	/10	
Bitter	/10	/10	
Umami	/10	/10	

Texture	Greatness	Crapiness	Write what changes you are going to do to get your animal wagging his tail
Crunch	/10	/10	
Creamy	/10	/10	
Smooth	/10	/10	
Soft	/10	/10	
Chewy	/10	/10	

The fact it there are lots of different textures. Just let your animal match the right texture to the right taste. The best way to figure out what works with what is to take your animal on a excursion of crunching and munching your way through great food with different tastes and textures.

Now for the question of colour, shape and smell. Well the Great Crap Test still applies. The only problem is there is unlimited combinations of colours, shapes and smells. With that in mind we don't have a book that is big enough to cover the whole spectrum. So, let's just stay with the basics. Besides if you want new ideas you just have to look them up on the net and then try them out with your animal being the ultimate decider.

Look at the table below to give you some ideas about colour and shape and smell. These will get you started but really there is an infinite number of smell combinations and sight combinations. Don't panic just trust your animal.

The Great Crap Test for The Eyes (Colour & Shape)			
Color	Greatness	Crapiness	Write what changes you are going to do to get your animal wagging his tail.
Red	/10	/10	
White	/10	/10	
Yellow	/10	/10	
Green	/10	/10	
Blue	/10	/10	
Brown	/10	/10	
Black	/10	/10	
Shape			
Square	/10	/10	
Circular	/10	/10	
Crescent	/10	/10	
Diamond	/10	/10	
Triangle	/10	/10	

Here is a bunch of smells to think about. See if you can think of some of your own.

The Great Crap Test for The Tongue (Taste & Texture)

Smell	Greatness	Crapiness	Write what changes you are going to do to get your animal wagging his tail.
Meaty	/10	/10	
Veggie	/10	/10	
Herbie	/10	/10	
Fruity	/10	/10	
Flowery	/10	/10	

Now here is a bonus Great Crap Test. This is about herbs and spices. One of the most creative cooks of all time would have to be the Colonel. Now you might think you know who I'm talking about, but I would have to deny it. You know it's a Code thing. So, this guy the Colonel said that food is the tool you use to deliver herbs and spices to the imagination. You see herbs and spices are the super stars when it comes to messing with the senses. So, take a tip from the Colonel. Master the craft of creating your own secret herbs and spices. Make it your signature. Mess with peoples, senses in a good way and it will really take your cooking to world leading popularity. Let's face that would be brilliant wouldn't it!

The Great Crap Test for The Taste Buds (Spice)

Spices	Greatness	Crapiness	Write what changes you are going to do to get your animal wagging his tail.
Meaty	/10	/10	
Veggie	/10	/10	
Herbie	/10	/10	
Fruity	/10	/10	
Flowery	/10	/10	

For completeness I've also thrown in a GCT for sound. Now here's the thing. You might not think that food and sound go together but they most certainly do. Think about it. The crack of pork crackle, the crunch of crispy skin salmon, the snap of fresh veggies and the sizzle of steaks and sausages. Who'd have thought that sound and food go so closely together. Of course, not all food has to have sound associated with it but for completeness we've thrown in this GCT for Sound.

Just a warning about sound, if your culinary creations start talking to you it's probably time to put down the red wine and toddle off to bed for the night. Otherwise have fun listening to the sound of your meals.

OB

The Great Crap Test for the Ears			
Master Blokes Mess with Your Senses			
David C			
Sound	Greatness	Crapiness	Write what changes you are going to do to get your animal wagging his tail.
Snap	/10	/10	
Crackle	/10	/10	
Pop	/10	/10	
Sizzle	/10	/10	
Crunch	/10	/10	

Try and think of some more of your own.

Smart Blokes Know How to Burn Things Properly

Your animal is versatile creature. It's able to help you out in a multitude of situations. From helping you decide if something is great or crap to whether it is cooked properly or not. However, to know if something is cooked properly or not, you need to understand that cooking is just a process of controlled burning. Cooking is the application of heat to food until it reaches the desired level of not quite completely burned. Scientifically speaking, whenever you apply heat to food, it begins the process of oxidization which is the fancy scientific name for burning. Therefore, if you think about it, cooking is just controlled burning. Which means when you are cooking you are really trying to reach the desired state between not burned at all and completely burned. Hence cooking is just controlled burning. Does that make sense?

Have a look at the table below and you'll see what I mean. When it comes trusting your animal to help you not quite burn things properly you need to use all your animal senses, so you can recognize the signs of too much or too little burning. While the stages of not too burned are pretty obvious to your animal the table below will help your head connect with your animal. Learn this well, so your animal can let your head know when to turn up the heat and when to turn it down. Have a look at the table below and get your head around it and it will all make the process of burning things properly make complete sense quickly enough.

No heat	Warming	Browning	Caramelising	Drying	Hardening	Charring of	Combustion
	Softening Slowly browning	Fluids rise	Sugars begin to soften and turn to toffee	Gases and fluids vaporise Proteins begin to bind	Proteins continue to bind Vapours continue to escape	Proteins and sugars begin to carbonize	The ignition temperature of the material is reached
Not burned at all	Early burning	Half way to burning Outside is burning; inside is just starting to think about it.	Well on the way to burning Burning on the outside and starting on the inside	Well burned on the outside Starting to burn on the inside as well	Just about burning on the inside as well	Early stage completely burned inside and out	Totally, completely burned Completely burned, up in flames, nothing but cinders

Of course, you need to know how to apply heat to the food, and that's easy enough; you already know most of it. You know how to turn the heat up and down, you just turn the knob, or move the slider if you have a fancy stove or oven. You already know how to put it in the cooker, turn the heat on, and then watch it, so you don't need to be taught anything so far. The real trick is to know when to turn the heat up, down or off.

You need to also understand when applying heat to food that food burns from the outside in (except in microwave cooking). This means that if you want to cook your food evenly throughout you must cook it slowly on a low heat with an all over heat source like an oven or a pot, steam, or pressure cooker. On the other hand, if you want to crisp up the outside and keep the inside relatively unburned, then you need to apply heat to the outside quickly before the inside begins to cook. In chef talk, this is called searing. For blokes, we like to call it browning or caramelizing. If you sear the outside and you then put it on a moderate heat, you can then get the insides up to the preferred level of not quite completely burned as well. Sounds tricky but after you've had a couple of goes at it you'll get the hang of it.

The trick with heat control is constantly ask your animal what he wants, then choose the setting from either high medium or low to suit. If he wants it crisp on the outside and rare in the middle, you will need a higher heat and shorter cooking time. If he wants it cooked evenly through, you will need a low to medium heat and a medium cooking time and probably an all over heat source. If, on the other hand, he wants it all falling apart and soft you will need a low heat and a very long cooking time and definitely an all over heat source like an oven or a pot. Too simple really!

Just a word of warning though. Every different type of protein, vegetable, dairy or liquid that you may want to cook will generally follow these rules, but the timing and intensity will change depending on the protein or the vegetable. But don't be dismayed. By learning to really think with your animal, you will very quickly work out the right way to apply heat to all the different foods you cook.

Have you ever notice what those chefs on TV do when they want to know if something is cooked properly or not? They look at it, they smell it, they touch it, taste it, and before that, they even listen to it.

Have a look at the table below and see if your animal can pick the different stages of burning using chef speak.

OB

Chef stages of not quite completely burned	Raw	Rare	Medium Rare	Medium	Well Done	Burning
Blokes stages of not quite completely burned.	Completely unburned	Early burning warming, softening sweating. Oxidizing and browning on the outside. Not a lot happening on the inside.	Almost half way to completely burned Oxidizing, Browning on outside softening stewing on the inside.	Half to completely burned. Oxidizing, caramelizing and charring on the outside, drying on the inside	Three quarters to completely burned. Gone paste caramelizing, well charred, dry as a dogs bone on the inside Start to worry	We have Ignition/ burning Oh, f%$&k This is where you begin to say oops f&%$k I've gone too b%^dy far, f$%k, f$%k, f$%k. Where's the bl$%dy sink? This is when it all goes to hell and back. Probably because you couldn't help yourself. You didn't listen to your animal. What can I say. You're a bloody sausage. Use the fire extinguisher and start again
Method	This one's tricky. Do nothing except put it on the plate and eat it.	Turn the heat on moderate to high. Put food on then whip it off before the burning gets a foothold. Repeat both sides.	Turn the heat on moderate to high. Put the food on and whip it off as soon as the juices rise. Then flip it over and repeat on the other side	Turn the heat on high to moderate. Put the food on, forget it's there, make a cuppa, the turn it when you smell the charring. Repeat for other side.	Turn the heat on moderate to high. Pour yourself a glass of red. Turn it after you've consumed half a bottle. Repeat for the other side. When finished throw it away.	Turn the heat on finish the bottle of red. Apply fire extinguisher, swear a bit. Start again, cancel the fire department. This time listen to your animal.
Example						

Hot and spicy prawn laksa
Can you feel your' animal
getting excited?

Black Fettuccini with steamed mussels herbs

Are you getting the sense of it?

Wanky Facts

All entertainment is about stimulatin the senses so that your imagination goe wow, you blood pressure and heart rate ris and your emotions go I love this.

A Moment in Cooking History

Spit roasting was used by peasants an Royalty alike throughout most Europea Empires.

The roast allowance for the court of Kin Henry the VIII on an average year wa 14000, large animals. This include everything from large animals like Oxe sheep and small animals like peacock and ducks. That's a lot of roasts.

Secret Women Business

Women love a bloke who has good senses

Imagination

The imagination's job is to see wow pictures in your head using what you already know so you can surprise the mind

(Leo DV)

"Smart blokes know magic is just a bluff that works"

Merl,
A bloke who's good with a trick or two,
from The Book of Legends

'Magic is what happens when the imagination is expressed effortlessly on the plate, and the mind goes wow.'

Leo, DV

Artist, architect, inventor, sculptor, creative genius, and uber-brilliant cook,

from The Book of Uber-Creative Blokes

Smart blokes know that magic is just a bluff that works

This book is called the Blokes' Guide to Brilliant Cooking. What we intend to do now is show you how to do just that, so you can put a total performance on the plate by bringing your imagination into the mix. The imagination's job in the brilliant cooking process is to build pictures in your head using what you already know; pictures which your animal gets all excited about. Now don't worry about whether you will go too big and ridiculous with your imaginings; just listen to and trust your animal, and you'll be right. Also, don't worry about how you're going to get the picture out of your head and into the world just yet. We will show you how to do that in the next chapter.

To understand how to get the picture in your head right and your imagination all fired up, you first must understand what creative blokes have known since „The 'Original Bloke' first crawled out of the rift valley, and that is „Magic is just a bluff that works'. What this means is that if you want to create magic that works, you have to work the bluff. Now, everyone knows that the secret of the bluff is in the details. But to get the bluff right you must know what you're trying to achieve with the bluff; otherwise, you run the risk of going all random. Now listen up, because this is important if you want to understand how to work the bluff effectively. You must understand that humans are just thinking animals. So, to get them all excited, you must stimulate their animal senses and surprise their animal mind so that their head goes„ "Wow, unbelievable, how did he do that".

Magic is what happens when you get the colours, the flavours, the textures, smells, and sounds right. It's what happens when you add a little surpise of the unexpected. When you get the details right the X factor cranks up the senses get stimulated, your animal gets excited and your head goes, Man, that was good! To get the details of the picture in your head right, remember to trust your animal and use the GCT.

I want to illustrate the idea that the magic of the bluff is in the details. If we start with the simplest detail of all, a name for example, which of these statements gets your animal all excited? 1. Robot from the future tries to kill boy, or 2. Terminator? no-brainer really!

Try this one, which of these two pictures grabs your imagination more? 1. A two-door car that is red or, 2. A low-profile, road-hugging red Italian sports car with calf-skin leather seats, a menacing black stallion on the bonnet, a grunting huge power unit, with a name like Ferrari F40.

Hard question isn't it? Der! What's interesting though, and this is the magic of the bluff, is that both statements are describing the same red car. One, you wouldn't notice if it hit you in the street, and the other one you would want to date if that sort of thing was allowed. Remember magic is just a bluff that works, and the magic of the bluff is in the details.

Yours

OB

How to get the picture in your head right.

Have a look at this plate; now imagine the most impressive meal you can on the plate, remembering you have to stimulate the senses and you have to surprise the imagination. What did you come up with? Did you struggle?

To help you get the picture in your head sorted, Leo one of the most imaginative and creative blokes of all time has come up with a set of planners that will take you step by step through the imaginary decision- making process and guarantees the picture you build on the plate on the table in your head is a total performance.

Remember what you're trying to do with your imagination; you're trying to build a picture in your head that will stimulate the senses and surprise the mind. So, the first step in getting the picture in your head right is to decide what's in it for the senses, and how you're going to surprise the mind. Don't forget that to get the balance right just keep asking your animal what he thinks.

The planner below helps you do this. When you get good at the imaginary part of brilliant cooking, you won't have to use the planners at all. The magic will just flow out of your head like it's supposed to. Don't worry about how you are going to cook it at this stage that is for the next chapter. For now, just get imaginative.

Pictures in your head planner

Creative Blokes See Pictures in Their Heads
Nostro D

What's in it for the imagination	Give it a theme,e.g., beef, chicken, spicy, asian, etc.	What's the surprise,e.g., stuffing, a secret flavour, extra crunch, and texture.	
What's in it for the eyes	Colour Think 3 colours at least	Presentation Simple, Zen, the Pack, and Stack	
What's in it for the ears	What does it sound like when you describe it, e.g., Lamb with red wine and twice baked veg.	Give it a fancy name, e.g., oven baked lamb in rich red wine sauce	
What's in it for the Nose	Smell meaty, rich red wine, veg		
What's in it for the tongue	Sweet	Sour	Savoury
	Salty	Spicy	Herby
	Pepper	Citrus	Meaty
What's in it for the touch	Tenderness Tender lamb,	Texture Smooth sauce Creamy vegetables with crispy skin	Moisture/dryness Moist

The next planner is a bit more, showy; it comes to you from a bloke who also knew a lot about being creative, his name was Will. Now if our Will knew anything, it was how to put a performance on, and in this case, his wisdom is going to help you put a performance on a plate. Remember using a planner is simply to help your imagination get started and to let you capture your ideas on paper so you don't forget them. You don't have to use the planners, but they will make the imaginary part of the whole brilliant cooking process simpler. For now, just get those imagination juices cranking.

The Performance on a Plate Planner

Learn to perform or get off the stage
Will S

Constructing an impressive performance	Write your decisions here
The Theme It's the theme of the show that gets the imagination interested. Think Asian, Italian, or think of a couple of your own like rich and spicy, meat lovers, or wine, beer, creamy, sweet go wild	
The Main Act Is? The main act is the star of the show. The main act is what everyone has come to see performed. It's what gets everyone excited. It could be a protein, e.g., fish, chicken, beef, etc., like Barramundi, Free Range, Wagyu. Or if you want go vegetarian soy, mushrooms, chickpeas	
The Support Acts Are? The support acts are there to make the main act look good. Usually veg but can be fruit or another type of protein. Ask your animal what he would like to eat with the main act.	
The Stage Dressings Are? The stage dressings set the scene and add colour and shape to the stage without making the show seem too busy and confusing. They include sauces, dressing, marinades, stuffing's, pastes, garnishes, dustings, drips, and drizzles. Remember to ask your animal to make sure you get the balance right.	
The Big Secret? The big secret is the twist in the plot that keeps the audience guessing. It keeps them coming back to try and figure it out. When it comes to cooking this is the secret combination of special herbs and spices (as the colonel used to say) that you put into the stage dressings or the sauces that gives the meal its flavour, colour, or texture X factor.	
The Presentation Style This is the look and feel of the show. The presentation style is lust for the eyes. It is the visual gin and tonic for a drinking audience. It could be modern, it could be rustic, and it could be artistic. Have a look at the next planner for ideas.	
The Fancy Name Will Be? The secret to a big first impression is to get the name right. A brilliant name gets the audience expecting to be impressed. It makes the audience want to watch the show	

The next planner will help you come up with some presentation ideas. Just look at the pictures, get the picture in your head and do what Miagi said, 'make like the picture'

Copyright Jim O'Connor

The Presentation Planner

The Plop and Drop

The Bonfire

The Zen

The Train Wreck

The Presentation Planner

The Butchers Window

The Toss

The Drizzle

The Drop

The Presentation Planner

The Dust

The Placement

The Pour

The Fancy Pattern

The Presentation Planner- Combos

The Splash, Place and Drop

The Pour Place and Drop

The Pour and Double Placement

The Double Placement Sprinkle and drizzle

Authentic Italian minestrone soup

Imagined by bloke

What's in It for the

Eyes,
Ears
Nose
Taste buds
Tummy

What's the

Main act
The Star Performer
The support act
The extras
The stage dressings
The big secret
The fancy name

Chinese noodles with prawns and sweet soy sauce

If you can imagine it, you can make it! But never forget what you're really imagining is a performance on a plate. You're always putting on a show?

Wanky Facts

Nothing exists in cooking that didn't first exist in a person's imagination.

It is impossible to navigate a room in the dark without imagination.

A Moment in Food History

Salt is the first form of food seasoning and was first consciously produced during the Neolithic period between 10,000 and 2,000 BC. Now that is a seriously popular product. Jim Morrison's favourite food was the humble Donair kebab with extra hot chilli and no tomatoes.

Secret Women Business

Women love a bloke who's imaginative!

Copyright Jim O'Connor

Heart

The hearts job is to bring the soul and make it all sing.
(Barry W)

"Uber-Master Blokes know the soul magic is in the heart"

Barry W
A Bloke who knew a lot about bringing the soul
From the book of Uber-Masters

Simple with Heart
is better than
perfect.

"The Heart brings it together

and makes it sing"

Barry
A bloke who knew a lot about bringing the soul
From the book of Uber-Master

Uber - Master blokes have "Heart"

Ok my friends, I need to make a bit of a gear change now. Where coming toward the end and I have one critical piece of bloke wisdom to share with you before we finish up. But, before I do, I must warn you. What I am about to share with you may disturb some, confuse some, while others it will excite. I also know that I'm about to strike few emotional notes and so for the more intellectual amongst you, you might want to look away from the book for a few minutes while I explain this to everyone else. Don't worry, you'll know when to look back and continue reading? So, for the intellectual types look away now. The rest of you pay attention.

There is one crucial secret in cooking in the way of the bloke that can't be ignored. In fact, it is a fundamental secret for being a completely well put together bloke. It is the quintessential secret that takes everything you do in life and living from great to extraordinary. It is the ingredient that brings all your thinking, imagining, instincts and efforts together and gives them a dose of super, un-believably, compelling, WOW!. This is the "Secret, Secret" that the Uber-Master blokes and for that matter the Uber-Master girls, have known since humans started creating stuff. It is the secret of Heart.

You must put your who you are-ness, your story, your pain, your passion, courage and soul into what you do if you want to take it to the Uber-Zone. Whether it be cooking, building, performing, decorating, parenting or painting nothing is truly great if it doesn't have "Heart".

So, what is "Heart"? It is everything we love, like, admire and desire about ourselves and others. It is the best of being human. It is our hopes and dreams, it is our optimism, courage, passion, history, story, challenges, all wrapped up and expressed on the plate. One of the most amazing things about humans is they can see "Heart" when it's there. They can also see when "Heart" is missing. Heart is the thing we long to see and the thing that we are amazed at when we see it. It's what we love, like, admire and desire to see and experience in everything we create.

If you want to know how to put heart into your culinary creations, it's simple really. But don't be fooled. Some of the simplest things to understand, are the hardest things to do. So how do you put "Heart" into your cookery? Simple, drop your guard, get out of your head and into your heart. Care for what you create and the people you are creating it for. Be, open, transparent, vulnerable to letting people see you in your creation. Have the courage to let who you are be reflected on the plate. Let the world see your story, your history, your thoughts, ideas, passions, loves and likes happen in front of them. Heart makes the imperfect, WAY better than perfect. Think about it.

OB

PS

Also, just a little reminder, don't get too upset when they love eating your heart on the plate, right there in front of you. It's kind of weird but necessary in cooking. It's not like you just want them to look and don't touch.

Heart It's the centre
of everything.

Drop your guard, have courage
and put yourself on the plate

Wanky Facts

It takes courage to have "Heart". Life is story so live a story you'd like to read. Humans love watching people who have heart

You know when you go into a museum and you see something and you love it. It's because you're mind and imagination are able to recognize the love that went into it.

The thing we all relate to in our Uber-Stars is heart. It's what sets them apart from the super stars.

A Moment in Cooking History

Chocolate was once used as a currency by the Aztecs. It was consumed as a bitter drink mixed with corn puree and spices.

The oldest evidence for soup is 6000 BC hippopotamus and sparrow meat soup. Ketchup was used as a treatment for diarrhea in the 1800's

Secret Women Business

Women love a bloke with heart

Hands

The hands job is to take everything the head, instincts,
imagination and heart want and construct it on the plate.
(Bob T B)

Real Blokes Don't Cook
They Construct

Bob T B
A real Mr Fix It
from the Book of Builders

Blokes don't cook, they construct.
Cookery is just a form of temporary
construction only with soft stuff.

Real Blokes don't cook, they construct

The single biggest mistake people can make when it comes to creating anything including a great meal is they aren't organised. This is where the head comes in. The head's job is to organise what you already know in an impressive way. To make the organisation process super easy to understand and follow, I am going to introduce you to a profound bit of bloke wisdom.

Smart blokes have always believed that cooking is just a temporary form of construction only using soft stuff. There really isn't any more to it. Start thinking this way, and suddenly, the whole process of cooking seems a lot less complicated, easy to follow and a much more doable. This piece of bloke's wisdom comes to us from one of the nicest blokes, you could ever hope to meet, and one of the greatest builders of all time: Bob. This is what Bob had to say about construction and cooking. It comes from The Book of Builders in "The Code".

> "Everything that is manmade (or woman or kid made to be fare) is constructed and cooking is no different. To know how to construct is to know how to cook. More to the point you only have to get your head around four steps to understand construction. In order to construct something; first you make a picture in your head, then thinking backwards work out the steps necessary to take the picture out of your head and into the world. After that you gather together some tools and a bunch of raw materials and clean, cut, mix, process and bolt them together until they look like the picture in your head. Finally, you polish and finish the final construction so that it looks all shiny and appealing.
>
> But be warned the real trick to constructing is to be organised otherwise you're risking an accident."

Bob
The ultimate Mr Fix it
from the Book of Builders

Doesn't sound too complicated does it? The first step in constructing is to get the picture in your head right. That's what the chapter on imagination was all about. You should be right on that count by now. Remember if you can close your eyes and figure out where the door is in your bedroom, you have more than enough imagination to do the picture in your head step. If you're worried, just trust the planners in the previous chapter. Or if you really want to live dangerously just trust your animal.

The thing about the picture in your head step is it's just dreaming if the pictures stay in your head. The trick now is to get them out of your head and into the world by working out the steps, the processes, the tools and the raw materials you need. To do this you need to master the most important of bloke arts and that is backward thinking. Genius blokes are naturally backward in their thinking.

Learning how to master backward thinking is the easiest and most effective way of getting your dreams to come true. As our Sherlock used to say clever blokes think backward.

By becoming a master of the fine art of backward thinking, you will simultaneously work out, the raw materials needed to construct your meal, the steps involved, the amounts and the timings as well as all the tools you need to get the job done.

Backward thinking is how you organize what you know into a construction process. Thinking backwards is simple enough. You start with the picture of what you want on the plate on the table in your head. Then ask yourself a simple question „What has to happen just before that to make that picture happen on the plate on the table in the world? and then write down your answer or just see it in your head and remember it if you want to truly cook without a net. Keep asking yourself the „What has to happen just before that?' question until you have worked out all the steps, you need to follow to get the picture out of your head and into reality.

Whether you write down the steps or not is up to you. Regardless of whether you write them down or not all you need to do now is add in amounts and throw in sometimes, temperatures and processes, and then if you turn the whole thing upside down, and run it forwards you've got yourself a master plan, including a raw materials list, a works schedule, a tools list, and a process schedule. In fact, if you think backwards properly you will have everything you need to do right in front of you beginning to end. The planner below shows you the stages of backwards thinking from the pictures in your head to the plate on the table. Now I know you've seen the backward thinking planner before in the section on thinking, so the one on the next page is one I already filled out. To make the backward thinking process easier, it helps to break it down into its natural stages. If you become familiar with this way of thinking, you will be able to do this on the fly, and you won't need to write things down. For now, however, writing things down makes organizing your thoughts a whole lot easier. You could use something like this, or you could do your own. Or if you really want to cook in keeping with the way of the bloke, you could do it all in your head as you go. But be careful with that one you might melt your C.P.U.

Yours

OB

PS

Have a look at this quickie head organiser, it's a bit simpler than the backward thinking planner.

The Quickie Head Organiser

Getting the picture in your head sorted.

Type of Protein	Write your answers here	How are you going to cook it	Tools you need	Times
1 Choose your protein				
2. Choose your veg				
3. Choose your sauce				
4. Choose your flavours				
5. Choose your textures				
6. Choose your herbs and spices.				

Production notes

Now have go at this backward thinking planner. Here is a live one to help you get your head around how to use it.

Backward thinking planner

The picture in your head	Processes	Tools and Materials
Scotch fillet and baked veg in spicy red wine sauce	Measure Clean Peel Chop Cut Gut Mix Cool Cook Place Plating Look Listen Taste	The requirements The tools The times The temps The raw materials Amounts

	The picture in your head	Processes	Tools and Materials
The table work	A beautifully cooked Scotch fillet, on a bed of winter veggies dripping with a perfectly balanced spicy red wine sauce, placed on the table, and happy customers	Place on the table with confidence; make sure you don't drop it. Sit down, smile, start chatting, eating, and drinking. Oh, also don't forget to listen girls love a bloke who listens to them.	Hands, table, girl, a big smile, a good conversation two seconds plus the rest of the night.
The plate work	See yourself assembling your beautiful meal from the plate up.	Bolt the materials together so that they look like the picture in your head. Place on plate according to the picture in your head: veggies, then meat, then sauce, then herbs. Put seasoning on. Put sauce on. Wipe the plate. Clean and polish the plate.	Picture in your head A plating area A cleaning cloth Seasoning Tongs, spoon, Timing 2 mins
The pre-plate work	Meat resting ready for plating, vegetables kept warm and moist ready for plating, sauces cooked and waiting for plating	Meat resting in pan, pan off the cooker turned off, oven turned off, veg ready to plate, sauces turned down too low	Bench for resting meat Oven Saucepan Fry pan 2 mins
The Hot Work Cold Work	The hot work cooking and under control	The hot work	Workspace, fry pan, oven, temp high med low depending
		Meat and/or veg in the	
		cooker cooking perfectly	
	Everything in the cooker is cooking	Temp and timer set. Sauces in pot cooking on mild heat.	

		Keep your ears, eyes, nose,	Set, timer set,
		and taste on the job.	Watch, listen,
The tool work	The cold work mixing and under control	The cold work	Touch smell, and taste
	Mixing the sauce, seasoning	Cut, mix, mash, chop Vegetables. Use your ears Eyes, nose, and taste.	
Pre-tool work	Get the tools ready, the power tools on standby, the oven warming, the hand tools ready, and the baking dish oiled ready for the veggies.	Set out tools close to hand, including bowls and bins for waste. Set oven temp, spray the baking tray, place veg- gies in tray. Get fry pan up to temp.	Fry pan, oven, vegetable oil, raw materials prepared, saucepan, tongs, knife
The bench work	Quantities measured, meat prepared, veg cut, sauces measured and mixed.	Clean, peel, cut, chop, veg- gies oiled ready for cooking. Quantities mixed together	Bench, knives, peelers, pots ready, bowls, vegetable oil, 20 mins
The pre-bench work	All raw materials sourced and laid out ready for bench work. Table set, room set up. Mood music organised	Go to the shop. Buy the stuff. Lay it out ready to use.	Money, shopping bag, car, a shop
The head work	Get the picture right in your head, Work out the master plan. Write a supplies list and works schedule.	Think a lot, write steps down, work out shopping list, timing list, quantities	A pen and paper, your In- stincts, imagination and your head.

Seared Salmon with capers and lemon butter sauce

Foundations first
Plate level
2nd level
3rd level
Dressings to finish
Too easy!

Wanky Facts

Nothing can be done in the kitchen without the hands apart from chatting and thinking. Your hands connect the mind and body to the world. Without hands it all stays in your head.

A moment in Cooking History

Antony Careme, notably the world's first celebrity chef was French chef and pioneered the creation of elaborate architecturally constructed meals known at the time as The Grande Cuisine. He lived between 1784 and 1833. It is believed the humble fortune cookie was invented by noodle maker, George Jung in 1916

Secret Women Business

Women love a bloke to be good with his hands.

Blokes Love Their Tools: Organizing the Tools

Fact is real blokes love their tools. Now you can go off and buy yourself a whole bunch of expensive fancy tools, but you don't have to really. People were cooking brilliantly well before fancy tools came along. Remember the kind of cooking you are going to do is using the skills you already have.

All a bloke needs are some cutters, gutters, cleaners, and peelers as well as some choppers, loppers, stabbers and some mixers, some bowls, some storer's, and pourers as well as some bashers, mashers, and crashers a few grippers, pots, pans, and plates for good measure.

Now you can do a lot of your cooking by hand, but at some point, you are going to have to apply some heat or cold, so there are a couple of power tools. A bloke must have some heaters and coolers, for example a hot plate, stove, oven, and griller, as well as a fridge and a freezer. If you like, you could also add in some power mixers, and power choppers, but really that's about all you will ever need. Have a look at the picture on the next page it's beautiful

Yours

OB

Organization.It's a beautiful thing

Organized tools reflect an organized mind.
An organized mind is an impressive thing.

Flour

Organizing the Processes

In keeping with the whole point of cooking the „way of the bloke' we are only going to use processes that you already know. But don't worry, you will still be able to churn out some serious food. When it all boils down to basics, cooking is just, cleaning, chopping, mixing, heating, cooling, and plating up food. There are whole bunch of fancy ways to do that, of course, but you don't need to be able to do much more than the basics to cook impressively. The following chart makes the cooking process super easy to follow in your head.

After you've had a look at it. You'll realize none of this seems too hard. So, who said cooking is difficult? It doesn't seem to be so far. Sure, Chef's do it all better and faster and easier but it's still pretty much the same cutting, chopping, mixing heating and cooling. In time you'll do it better, faster, easier. Now remember I'm not saying Chef's don't have super fancy processes. They do. For you though, you'll be right with these.

When you think about it, the kitchen is the cooking work site. Now to fully understand the rules about how best to organise the kitchen, you can have a look at the section at the back of this book called „The Kitchen'.

When you set up the work site, think of the layout of your kitchen as a production line and each zone represents different parts of the production process. In simple terms, you must have an area for your raw materials and area for your tools, and area for the bench work, cleaning, mixing, cutting, gutting, and chopping. You need an area for the hot and cold work as well as a place to plate up. Of course, don't forget to have a waste system close to hand as well. In an ideal kitchen all these separate sites need to be close to hand but clearly separated. Nothing is worse than you chopping site getting mixed up with your blending, or your blending getting mixed up with your waste disposal.

Don't worry if you can't figure out a process. If you get stuck, ask yourself a slightly different question, "how can I use what I already know to make what I want, or something just as good, happen? If you can't answer that question, then you're trying to overcomplicate things.

For information about temps and timings, you can find that information out anywhere. However, as a rule of thumb when working with heat you only need to know low, medium and high. For timing just look it up. Or if you really want to go instinctive, just trust your animal.

Yours'

OB

The Cooking Processes

The pre-bench work	1. Getting the picture in your head right 2. Make a works schedule 3. Source the raw materials 4. Source and organize the tools 5. Setting up the site
The bench work	1. Cleaning 2. Peeling 3. Gutting 4. Cutting 5. Mixing 6. Managing the waste

The power work	The hot work	1. Check the chart 2. Turn the temperature on/off, down/up 3. Keep an eye on it
	The cold work	1. Put it in the fridge/freezer 2. Keep an eye on it 3. Take it out of the fridge/freezer
The plate work	The plating work	1. Look at the plating picture 2. Make like the plating picture 3. Cleaning and polishing, making it shiny

The table work	4. Put it on the table with a smile 5. Sit 6. Eat 7. Chat 8. Drink

Steak in spicy red wine and pepper sauce with roast mushrooms and potatoes

Build it like a bloke
Lay the foundations,
Lay the first level
Lay the second level
Lay the top level

Then add the finishing touches with a bit of something special

Rare roast beef with crispy winter veg and rich tomato sauce

Built by bloke

Wanky Facts

All brilliant efforts require high level organization. Cooking is just organizing food for eating. Brilliant cooking requires high level organization.

A moment in cooking history

In the late 1700's Antonin Careme created desserts based on elaborate architectural design and made garnishment and plate presentation an art form. The earliest archaeological evidence for the consumption of soup dates back to 6000bc and appears to be hippopotamus.

Secret Women Business

Women love a bloke who can organise stuff

The Kitchen

The Kitchen's job is to be the site / place where the hands bring it all together.
Henry F

"Wise blokes understand,
happy site happy life

Henry F
A legendary bloke and master of the work site
From the book of builders

The kitchen is where the hands connect the food to the head, instincts, imagination, heart on the plate

The Hot work

Wise blokes understand happy site happy life

Let's get our head around what the kitchen really is for a bloke who wants to be a brilliant cook. It's your work site. It's where you create your culinary dreams. It's your playground. It's your laboratory where you experiment with your new ideas. It's a place where a creative bloke can go and be happy, find solitude and contentment as he develops his cooking wizardry. Unfortunately, it could also be a place of great heartache, a cauldron of pain and suffering a catastrophe in the making or a place when you become crushed on the rocks of cooking disasters.

There is something that you can do to tip the balance in your favour, however. The trick is to fully understand the meaning of the next secret of cooking „the way of the bloke', and that secret is „Wise blokes know happy site happy life'. You see it's pointless having the best instincts, the greatest processes, and brilliant imagination if your hands can't bring all that into being because your site „ain't right'.

Probably the single most important skill of impressive cooking is „organisation'. Probably the single biggest mistake a cook could make is to not be organized. So, in keeping with this idea, we are going to show you how to simplify your site so that your cooking organization just flows. To keep this idea simple think of it simply as this;

"Organise the work site so the work site organizes you".

Henry, F
A legendary bloke and master of the work site
from the book of builders

You've got to have the space, the tools, and the materials organised and ready so that everything flows. Now don't get all panicky and scared just because you've never been organised a day in your life because greater blokes than you or I have already come up with a system that will make it all super easy. Just get ready to organise the work site so the work site organizes you

Think of a work site as made up of a series of work zones or mini work sites. If you do this well the cooking process will seem simple, un-confusing and it will all just flow. The trick is to have a zone set aside for each part of the cooking process when you set up the site. It is best if they don't overlap, however if you have a small space that's ok. In a small kitchen simply use bowls, trays and cutting boards to differentiate the different parts of the site. Remember, an organized site stops you getting confused and keeps the production line flowing.

On a building site, you have five basic zones. These are the martialing area, the pre-production area, the production zone, the assembly and finishing area, and the waste zone. The martialing area is the zone where the raw materials and your tools are gathered and wait until they are needed. This is usually out of the way but within arm's reach to avoid you having to jog around the site.

The pre-production zone is where the raw materials go through their early preparation; they get trimmed, cleaned, chopped to size, heated up, or cooled down, and so on, ready for production. Usually the sink, and a chopping area.

The production zone is the assembly area or the place where all the pre-produced materials get turned into the finished product. This is usually the place where all the mixing, heating, and cooling is done. Usually stove tops, ovens and grillers as well as fridges, freezers and power mixing places.

The assembly and finishing area is where the cooked materials are plated up, and the plates are cleaned, and the meals are finished. This is usually clean flat surface but not the floor. It puts people off when their food is plated up on the floor. A table or bench will do nicely.

The waste sites. On most work sites there are two main waste sites. The site close to the work in the kitchen this is usually a bowl for waste close to the chopping action. Then there is the main waste dump. You guessed it the bin.

Have a look at the pictures on the next few pages and you will see what I mean. But remember the two golden rules of setting up the work site. The first is "Organize the site so the site organizes you". The second is a profound bit of bloke wisdom, and it is this, "Wise blokes know, happy site, happy life"

OB.

Site Planner

Site	Site Activities	Requirments
Planning Site	Sit, think backwards Write it all down.	Chair, pen your favourite beverage.Time
Pre-Prep Site	Unpacking	Raw Materials
	Standing aside	Space
	Get rid of waste	Waste Site
		Tools Site
Prep Site	Cold work	Boards
	Hot work	Chopping Space
	Pre-Construction	Clear Space
	Get Rid of Waste	Waste Site
Fabrication Site	Bending	Mixing Site
	Mixing	Heating site
	Heating Coolling	Cooling site
	Combining	Combining site
	Get rid of waste	Waste Site
Plating Site	Constucting	Plates
		Space
		Finese
Polishing and Finishing Site	Polishing	Towel
		Wipers

Have a look at the photos on the next few pages and you'll get the idear

Copyright Jim O'Connor

Happy site happy life

Cold Work

The chopping,
blending and
mixing site

Organise the
site so the site
organises you

An organized site is good for the soul

It is where brilliance is prepared

Cold Work

The plating, polishing and finishing site.

Where dreams are plated

Pre-Plating site

And Greatness created

Nothing is better than

an organised site

The Presentation Site

Wanky Facts

Nothing gets done, created or comes into being without organization of raw materials and or people within the same space at the same time. Life is of lessons in how to organize people and materials into what we want.

A Moment in cooking history

The most expensive coffee in the world is Kopi Luwak and comes from Sumatra in Indonesia. The coffee e beans are harvested from Civet pooh after it has eaten ripe coffee beans

Secret Women Business

Women love a bloke who's good in the kitchen.

Mastery

"Head, instincts, imagination and heart
are nothing without practice.
(Mas O)

"Master Blokes have a go. Uber Master Blokes have a go and hit repeat fearlessly!"

Mas. O
An Uber Legendary bloke who know a lot about using his hands
from the book of Masters

Rack of Lamb and roasted winter
vegetables with red wine sauce

Master Self

Master Cooking

Master Life

Beautiful!

This is Very Good. Now Do it again!

Master blokes have a go and hit repeat

Getting your head right by believing you know enough, thinking backwards, constructing a meal, are essential or you won't even start your journey to impressing through brilliant cooking. Tapping into your imagination is the only way to create the brilliance you're looking for as you become brilliant at cooking.

Learning to trust your animal instincts is about learning to make all those critical judgments that are necessary to bring everything together in the right way and in the right balance. Putting Heart into your cooking is essential to make your meals compelling. But it's all just a big fat fairy tale in your head if it stays there, which means that until you have a go and get right into the doing you're just dreaming.

Let me remind you what Antony C said at the start of this book. „Brilliant cooking is what happens when you connect your head, instincts, imagination, and your heart, to your HANDS in the kitchen.' It's in the doing that all the connecting happens; without the hands doing the do there can be no connecting, without the connecting there can be no brilliance and no mastery. The trick then to becoming a master is to do it and keep doing it until you do it well, then keep doing it until you have become a master of doing it well. Then keep doing it until you become a master of doing masterfully

It's in having the courage to have a go that you must to pull your head, instincts, imagination, and heart together. So, just have a go, experiment and learn what works from what doesn't. The secret I am passing on here is simple. Master blokes have a go and hit repeat. One of the greatest Master Blokes, in fact a truly Uber-Master was Mas O. a legend amongst men and a bloke who really knew what it meant to use his hands, said, "have a go and hit repeat". In fact, he said the way to mastery is to do something masterfully a thousand times. Only then will you learn to trust your head, your instincts, imagination and heart, unquestioningly and without pause or concern.

But a word of warning, only impressive blokes should have a go at „the doing' because it takes courage, humility, fierce determination, and a willingness to fall over, make mistakes, learn from them, get up, and keep doing the do. You must be a student of cooking „the way of the bloke' to become a Bloke Master.

Life is just a great big lesson. Mastering life begins with being humble enough and willing to master the lessons. Nothing could be truer than in the chaotic world of the kitchen. The person who embraces the "have-a-go" philosophy will have fun as they learn to be a brilliant cook. The person who is frightened of mistakes, or is too scared to take risks, will learn nothing and create nothing. The secret of the Master is they know that they are simply a student.

Are you ready be a student of the way of the Bloke and just have a go? Are you ready to learn how to cook „the way of the bloke' and be humble enough to learn from your mistakes as well as your successes? Are you ready to back yourself and develop a style that is entirely your own? Are you ready to live dangerously and cook without a net, trusting your head, instincts, your imagination, and your heart to tell your hands what to do?

If you are, then get cracking and have a go. If you aren't ready for bloke mastery, then it's ok. We understand being a full bloke can be intimidating.

Yours

OB

"A Master bloke knows the hands
bring the whole show together.
An Uber-Master Bloke knows
repetition makes the master"

Mas O

"The Master gets excited because they know they are a student."

Philip S
A seriously Zen Bloke
From the Book of Masters

Wanky Facts

The human brain is like a biological computer that is programmed through repetition. What you repeat you master for good or ill?

A moment in Cooking History

Perpetual stew was a common way of cooking in throughout Europe's medieval inns. A pot was hung over a fire and was constantly replenished. It would often be days or weeks before the pot was emptied or cleaned.

Secret Women Business

Women love a bloke who masters his own destiny

The Challenge

Brilliantly Simple. Simply Brilliant

Secret Women Business
Women love a Bloke Who Can Cook

Super-Secret
Women love their bloke to be brilliant and impressive.

The Challenge. Are You Up for It?

There you have it. The full explanation of „Brilliant Cooking the Way of the Bloke' as described in „The Code' and a few bits of advice about how to impress women. The only thing that remains now is to ask you if you are ready to meet the challenge. Are you ready to go into some kitchen anywhere in the world armed with nothing more than your instincts, your imagination, your head, and your hands and create your own brilliant meals. If you are, then that is well and good. If not that's OK, we won't tell anyone.

Oh, also could you please make sure that don't pass these secrets on to the women folk. Remember „The secrets you have read here have been kept secret for a very long time, and we hope to keep them secret for another very long time.'

Yours sincerely

OB

Step	Summary of the step
Step 1.	Trust you know enough.
Step 2.	Remember to trust your animal and use the GCT throughout the whole process. Your animal knows best.
Step 3.	Use your imagination to get the pictures right in your head and add some magic. Use the planners to keep track or do it without a net
Step 4.	Use backwards thinking to work out the steps, the materials and the processes you need to make it all happen. Get the tools and raw materials together.
Step 5.	Organise the site so the site organizes you.
Step 6.	Have a go. Let your hands bring it all together
Step 7.	If the food on the plate on the table is as good or better than the food on the plate on the table in your head, then be happy. If not go back, ask your animal what happened then start again.
Step 8.	Keep having a go until you have Mastered using your instincts your imagination, heart and your head to connect to your hands in the kitchen!' Keep having ago because that's "The Way of The Bloke"

PS

Remember, to trust The Code,
Always Trust the Code